The World of Caves, Mines and Tunnels

Stephen Hoare

MACDONALD YOUNG BOOKS

First published in Great Britain in 1999 by Macdonald Young Books

© Macdonald Young Books 1999
Text © Stephen Hoare 1999

Macdonald Young Books, an imprint of Wayland Publishers Limited
61 Western Road
Hove
East Sussex
BN3 1JD

Find Macdonald Young Books on the Internet at http://www.myb.co.uk

Commissioning Editor: Fiona Courtenay–Thompson
Project Editor: Lisa Edwards
Designer: Chris Leishman
Picture Researcher: Shelley Noronha
Illustrator: Bruce Hogarth
Borders illustrated by: Peter Bull Studios
Cover illustrated by: Colin Sullivan

Photograph acknowledgements:
The Bridgeman Art Library: p28(c), p37(cl); Camera Press: p35(tl); J Allan Cash: p13(tr); Mary Evans: p17(tr); G.S.F. Picture Library: p11(tc); Hulton Getty: p31(tr); Impact: p13(b), p25(br); Imperial War Museum: p30(bl); M.R.P. Photography: p23(cr); Öresundkonsortiet: p41(b); QA Photos: p38(cr), p43(b); Tony Stone: p8(l), p15(br); Topham: p42(cl); Wayland: p32(bl); Zefa: p24(cl).
Source for illustration on p32 – People's Army of Vietnam and US Army Records

The author and publisher would like to thank the following for their assistance:
Maurice Jones, *Tunnels and Tunnelling*
Trimble Navigation Limited (GPS Systems)
Ben Roskrow, *Housebuilder*
Gordon Wiseman, *Railway Gazette*
Mike Woof and Kieran Castile, *World Mining Equipment*

A CIP catalogue for this book is available from the British Library.

Printed and bound in Portugal by Edições ASA

ISBN: 0 7500 2255 8

Contents

Mines

Tunnels

The Amazing Underworld

The world beneath our feet is a magical and mysterious place. The Ancient Egyptians, Greeks, Romans and Vikings all believed in gods of the underworld. Their myths helped them to explain the unknown – why water bubbled up out of the ground, why volcanoes erupted, and why precious minerals were found underground.

The Fires of Hell

Ancient peoples often believed that the underworld was a threatening place. Red-hot molten rock and lava bursting to the earth's surface were thought to be a sign that the gods were angry. The medieval myth of the fires of Hell was probably based on early volcanic activity. Likewise, the Norse legend about a fire-giant setting the earth ablaze is said to be based on the eruption of an Icelandic volcano, Mount Hekla.

The Pu'u O volcano erupting at Kilauea in Hawaii, USA.

The underworld was a place of darkness, mystery but also peace. Brimming with deep lakes and still caverns, for many ancient peoples it was a place to rest in when you died. In Ancient Egypt, people worshipped Osiris, god of the underworld. When a king or queen died, Osiris judged whether they were fit to enjoy an afterlife in the underworld. This is why the Egyptians buried their pharaohs in deep, underground chambers (see page 15).

Mythical Underworld

In Ancient Greek mythology, Hades, the god of the Underworld, lived in a huge cave beyond the River Styx. The entrance to the Underworld was guarded by a three-headed, fire-breathing dog called Cerberus. The Greeks believed that Hades created winter by capturing the goddess Persephone, and taking her to live in his underground kingdom.

Solid metal inner core
(1,370 km deep)

Liquid metal outer core
(2,000 km deep)

Stony mantle
(2,900 km deep)

The outer layer
or lithosphere,
is made up of the
crust and part of the
upper mantle

The Real Underworld

Today, engineers have learned to tunnel and mine deep underground, and potholers have explored some of the earth's deepest caves. We know that when a volcano erupts or when an earthquake rumbles it is not a sign from the gods. It is simply pressure building up inside the earth's molten core. This cross-section shows the layers of matter contained inside the earth.

Some caves are places where miracles are believed to happen. The underground spring at Lourdes in southern France is a place of pilgrimage. In 1858, the Virgin Mary is said to have appeared to a fourteen-year-old girl called Bernadette Soubirous in a grotto there. The spring water is said to cure illness and disability.

Find out how big a part the underground world has played throughout history in the pages that follow. Discover exactly how and why people have mined it, lived in it, fought from it, and travelled through it, from prehistory to the present day.

CAVES
Caving In
Exploration

Caves are among the last unexplored places on earth. They are thousands and even millions of years old. Many caves were formed after the last great Ice Age, when torrents of water from the melting ice caps created waterfalls, valleys and lakes. The biggest caves are found in limestone, where water trickling through the porous rock has eroded vast underground systems.

The water that trickles through limestone is actually a weak acid, made from rainwater and carbon dioxide from the air and soil. Over thousands of years, the acid eats away at the rock until caves are formed. This acid also leaves deposits of natural chemicals called minerals. These eventually form hanging 'icicles' of rock called stalactites.

Caves were vitally important to the early humans who gathered in the entrances to shelter from the winter cold. These people cooked and kept warm by the fireside, but they also journeyed deep inside the caves to perform strange rituals and ceremonies.

Going Down

Some people explore caves for a hobby. Cavers, or potholers as they are sometimes called, carry rope and climbing gear, and also wear safety harnesses and helmets in case of falling rocks. Entering a cave is sometimes like being lowered down a well. Many caves are blocked by rocks and mud and are barely wide enough for a person to squeeze through. A caver anchors a rope to a spike hammered into the rock near the mouth of the pothole. He then lowers himself down on a line attached to a safety harness. Where a cave is completely submerged in water, cavers have to wear rubber wet suits and face masks and breathe through oxygen tanks.

Cave Art

Cave paintings have been found all over the world including Spain, North Africa, North America and Australia. The oldest-known rock art – a series of engraved circles – was discovered at a site on the Kimberley Plateau of Western Australia in 1996. It is believed to be 76,000 years old.

The Lascaux caves contain some of the best Stone Age paintings ever found in Europe. There are pictures of wild horses, woolly mammoths, lions, antelopes and bison. The paintings were made between 30,000 BC and 10,000 BC.

Archaeologists have found other forms of cave art, from figures and animals moulded in clay to rock carvings and engravings of animals.

Archaeologists believe that cave paintings possessed a special significance for the people that made them. It is possible that if an animal was drawn, it meant that its spirit was captured. Perhaps the next time a hunt took place, people believed that the drawn animal was easier to kill.

Holed Up
Cave Dwelling

From the very dawn of human life to the present day, people have made use of caves. Early tribes used rock shelters to keep dry and warm in winter and cool in summer. The earliest-known cave dwellers lived in grottos at Vallonnet on the Mediterranean coast of France 950,000 years ago. People first inhabited the Zhoukhoudian caves in China, a vast network of limestone caverns 175 metres long, 700,000 years ago.

Settled in Stone

Some of the earliest dwellings were man-made caves. In North America, the Pueblo Indians of Colorado built stone huts inside the entrances of caves and in the hollows of overhanging cliffs. The Pueblos take their name from the Spanish word for 'town' or 'village'. At the Mesa Verde pueblo, the Indians lived in a massive complex of buildings as much as four storeys high. This picture shows how Mesa Verde might have looked when people lived there over 1,000 years ago.

Apartment building – each apartment usually had 1 living room and 2 storerooms

Security watchtower – the highest building, used to look out for enemies approaching

Kiva – a circular underground room, probably used for religious and other ceremonies

Courtyard – a communal area probably used for preparing food or making tools and household objects

Sipapu – a hole in the floor of the Kiva, thought to be an entrance to the spirit world

The Stone Age builders of Skara Brae, on the island of Orkney off the coast of Scotland, excavated soil to build their circular stone huts underground. With only a small amount of wall showing above ground, the huts were roofed with flat stone slabs. These were then covered over with soil to keep their inhabitants snug against the bitterly cold North Sea winds.

It is thought that the huts at Skara Brae in Scotland were built in around 2000 BC.

Subterranean Shopping

If your winters are freezing cold and the snow falls in blizzards, where better to shop, eat or go to the movies than underground? In Canada, Montreal has a city centre that is deep below the high-rise office blocks and streets. The labyrinth of underground passages and shopping malls stretches 31km. Underground City has its own subway train stations and over 1,600 shops, 200 restaurants and 30 cinemas. There are also underground hotels and apartment blocks, so that the people who live or stay there need never come up to the surface.

Cool Down Under

Coober Pedy in South Australia is a tiny mining township in the desert. Around 4,000 people live there – mainly opal miners and their families. In summer, temperatures soar well above 30°C. But this does not trouble many of the town's inhabitants – they live underground. Up to 15 metres below ground, converted opal mines make ideal homes. With air supplied from a ventilation shaft and piped running water, these underground homes are cool and dry.

"When you're digging out your home you might find some more opals which can help pay for it. People like their dug-outs – you can whitewash the walls and carpet the floors. And part of the house is on the surface – that's where you'd store your water in a tank and park your car."
Mary, a miner's wife from Coober Pedy.

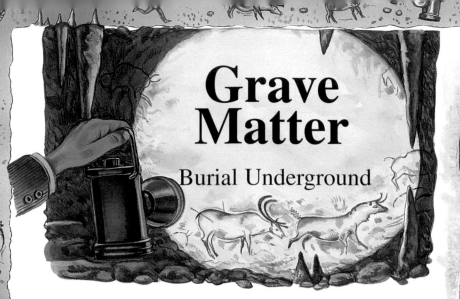

Grave Matter

Burial Underground

From prehistoric times, people have developed rituals for burying their dead underground. The earliest-known burial took place 50,000 years ago. The body of a man was discovered in a shallow grave deep inside the Shanidar cavern of northern Iraq.

Catacombs

Underneath the city of Rome lies a maze of underground passages. Built between AD 150 and AD 400, these are the catacombs where early Christians buried their dead. At the time, it was illegal to dig graves inside the city walls but people were allowed to bury their dead in tunnels outside it. The bodies were placed in lead coffins or simply wrapped in linen shrouds and stored on ledges cut into the walls of the catacombs. Over 750,000 bodies are buried here.

Barrows

About 3,000 years ago, Iron Age people buried their dead in long chambers covered with earth. These mounds or 'barrows', were made up of an arch of huge standing stones, capped with a flat slab.

Some barrows were built for one important person. This cross-section shows a collective barrow with small tombs along its sides.

A large stone was used to seal the entrance of the barrow

The stones were covered over with earth, but a tunnel was left so that bodies and grave offerings could be placed inside the stone tomb. Afterwards, the entrance of the tomb was filled in with earth and rocks. These burial mounds can be found all over Europe.

Rock Tombs

In 1922, an archaeologist called Howard Carter discovered the tomb of Tutankhamun in the Valley of the Kings in Egypt. The 18-year-old boy-king had died more than 3,000 years ago. It took workers two weeks to dig out a flight of twelve steps leading down into a complex of passages and chambers. The Ancient Egyptians worshipped Osiris, god of the underworld, and believed that people would have an 'afterlife' in his underground kingdom.

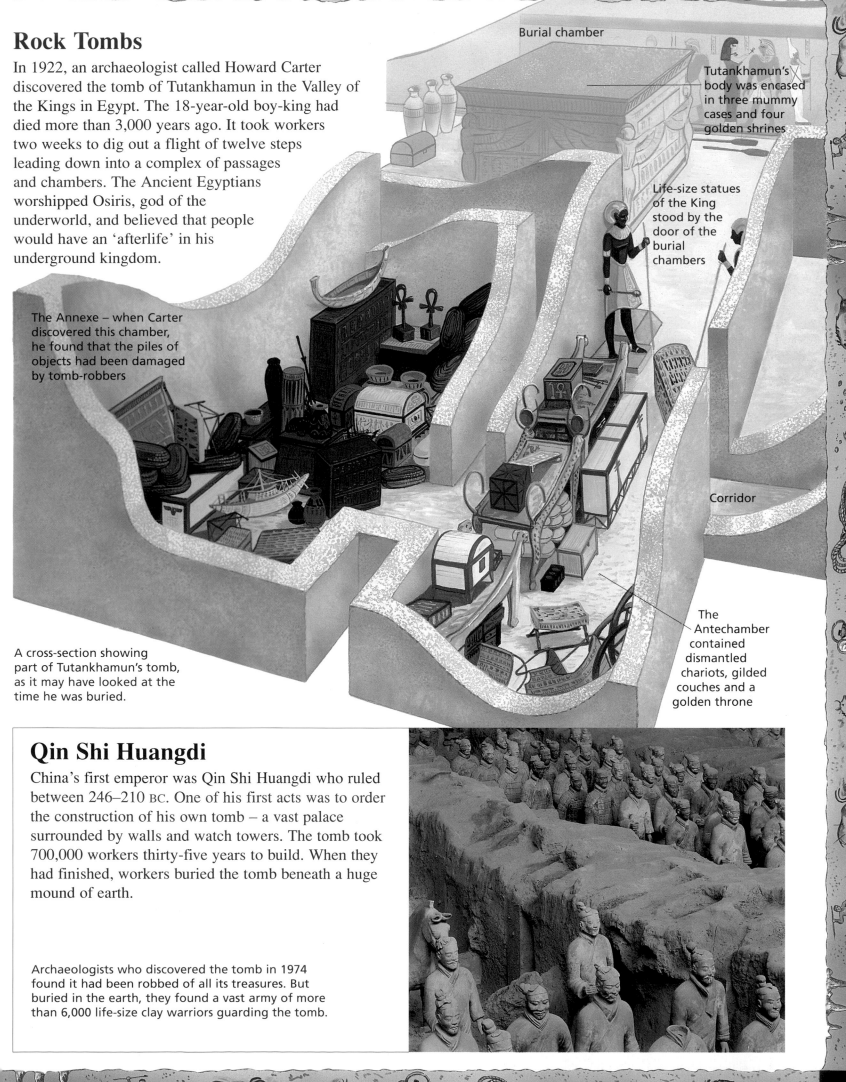

Burial chamber

Tutankhamun's body was encased in three mummy cases and four golden shrines

Life-size statues of the King stood by the door of the burial chambers

The Annexe – when Carter discovered this chamber, he found that the piles of objects had been damaged by tomb-robbers

Corridor

A cross-section showing part of Tutankhamun's tomb, as it may have looked at the time he was buried.

The Antechamber contained dismantled chariots, gilded couches and a golden throne

Qin Shi Huangdi

China's first emperor was Qin Shi Huangdi who ruled between 246–210 BC. One of his first acts was to order the construction of his own tomb – a vast palace surrounded by walls and watch towers. The tomb took 700,000 workers thirty-five years to build. When they had finished, workers buried the tomb beneath a huge mound of earth.

Archaeologists who discovered the tomb in 1974 found it had been robbed of all its treasures. But buried in the earth, they found a vast army of more than 6,000 life-size clay warriors guarding the tomb.

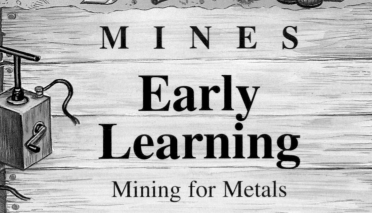

MINES
Early Learning
Mining for Metals

Pure forms of metal – gold, silver, copper, tin, lead and iron – occur naturally in rock. This metal-rich rock is called ore. Early people first discovered gold, silver and tin on stream beds, where small pieces of ore-rich rock had been washed by water and then mixed with mud and sand.

Bronze-Age smelters at work

The First Miners

Primitive people prized gold and used it to fashion decorative objects and jewellery. In around 6000 BC, people discovered that if you light a fire beneath certain rocks, the metal within them melts and trickles out. Early miners created big furnaces out of charcoal to 'smelt' the ore that they dug out of the ground. As the metal started to melt it was collected in trays called 'ingots'.

A major discovery occurred in around 3700 BC when people found that if tin and copper were mixed, the result was an alloy (a mixture of metals) called bronze. This was a hard, heavy material that proved ideal for making weapons that were far superior to existing flint ones.

The use of bronze became widespread in around 2000 BC at the start of the Bronze Age. This valuable metal opened trade routes across the world. It was smelted across Europe, China, Central Asia, and North and South America.

Ancient Miners

The Ancient Romans and Egyptians mined and smelted tin, copper, lead and iron. The Romans used picks to break up soft rock, and fire to make hard rock split and fracture. The Egyptians used wood to split rock; wedges were driven into cracks in the stone and soaked with water until they expanded and split the stone.

Medieval Miners

Medieval miners were the first people to venture underground to mine for metals. They went down deep shafts and tunnels on ladders, using picks and hammers to hack away at the rock. They shovelled the ore into baskets that were winched to the surface on ropes.

German scholar De Agricola wrote a book called *De re metallica* in 1556 on mining methods. It contained pictures like this one, depicting early mining techniques.

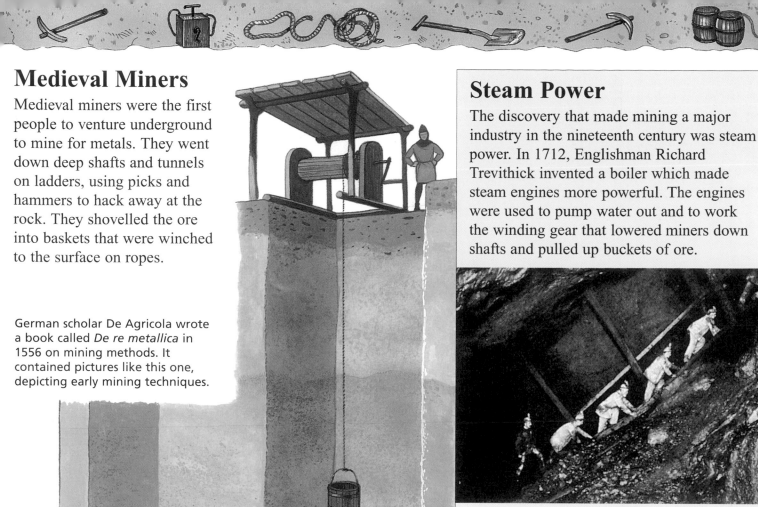

Gunpowder revolutionized mining when it arrived in the West from China during the Middle Ages (c.AD 400–1200). To clear big areas of rock, miners laid explosive charges in crevices. These were lit with a fuse made of a single straw filled with gunpowder. Deep underground, mine tunnels had to be held up by wooden props to prevent the roof caving in.

Steam Power

The discovery that made mining a major industry in the nineteenth century was steam power. In 1712, Englishman Richard Trevithick invented a boiler which made steam engines more powerful. The engines were used to pump water out and to work the winding gear that lowered miners down shafts and pulled up buckets of ore.

This picture shows tin miners in Cornwall, England. Miners had to climb up a series of mine shafts until engines were invented with enough power to hoist them up to the surface of the pit.

Metal Matter

The patron saint of tin, St Piran, was a sixth-century monk who lived in Cornwall in England. According to legend, a white cross appeared in a rock slab when Piran lit a fire. The fire had melted veins of tin inside the rock. Tin from Cornwall was being traded as long ago as 1000 BC.

During the Californian gold rush of 1849, more than 80,000 prospectors headed west across America to dig for gold. They used pans to sieve the mud on the river bed, and miners dug out rock with picks. Small mining camps soon became bustling towns overnight.

Open Mined

Opencast Mining

Deep in the heart of Nevada's White Pine County in the USA, the BHP mining company digs for copper. Robinson Mine has been operating for over a century, but it is no ordinary mine. The topsoil – called the overburden – has been removed from the side of a mountain to reveal the ore. This is a giant 'opencast' mine.

Underground mines can only make a profit if the extracted ore is high grade (almost pure) and the production rate is high. Robinson's ore is low grade, containing as little as 1% copper. So it has to be dug out of the ground on a large scale that is not possible underground. Each year, Robinson Mine produces 73,000 tonnes of copper and its earthmoving machines shift up to 7 million tonnes of rock.

The Robinson Mine is a huge pit with a series of steps or benches that descend down the side of the mountain. Big 'drag roads' used by heavy machines connect the benches.

Boulder-blasting

The first stage in the mining process is to bore deep holes in the side of the mountain to take explosives. This is done with drilling rigs. Blasting takes place once or twice a week and it can bring down as much as 300,000 tonnes of rock in one fall.

Drilling rig

Next, a giant 980-tonne electric shovel scoops the boulders up in its bucket, lifting as much as 40 cubic metres of rock at a time. Rocks are then loaded onto a huge, 240-tonne dump truck.

Shovel and dump truck

Satellite Tracking

Drilling into the rock for blasting calls for great precision. Explosive charges must be placed very precisely to bring down the rock in the right place. The position of the drilling rig is controlled by an on-board computer (a global-positioning system or GPS) that calculates its exact position by satellite radio beams.

Copper Facts

◆ Copper is first believed to have been used to make simple tools by people in around 8000 BC.
◆ Humans discovered how to melt and shape copper from about 6000 BC.
◆ The Ancient Egyptians were mining copper from around 3000 BC.
◆ Most of the world's mined copper is used by the electrical industry because it conducts electricity better than any other metal.
◆ 70% of the world's known reserves of copper are found in seven countries: Chile, the U.S., Russia, Zaire, Peru, Zambia and Mexico.

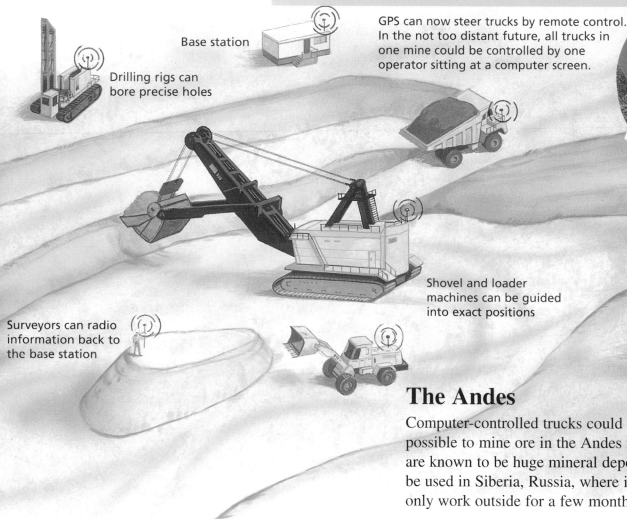

Base station

Drilling rigs can bore precise holes

GPS can now steer trucks by remote control. In the not too distant future, all trucks in one mine could be controlled by one operator sitting at a computer screen.

Machines can locate the highest-grade ores very quickly

Shovel and loader machines can be guided into exact positions

Surveyors can radio information back to the base station

The Andes

Computer-controlled trucks could one day make it possible to mine ore in the Andes mountains, where there are known to be huge mineral deposits. They could also be used in Siberia, Russia, where it is so cold people can only work outside for a few months of the year.

Crushing and Refining

1. Rocks are taken to an on-site crushing plant where they are broken up into pieces the size of a pea.

2. The gravel is put through a mill where it is ground finer than sand.

3. Copper is extracted by a process called flotation. As water is passed through the gravel, the fine sand turns to mud and tiny particles of copper float to the surface in bubbles.

4. The copper is taken by rail to a 'smelter', where it is melted in a furnace and then moulded into sheets.

5. The sheet metal is dipped in a special bath which passes an electric charge through it. Pure copper is deposited on the electric terminal.

6. Valuable by-products are removed at this stage – any gold and silver found with the copper can now be separated out.

Pitfalls

Mining For Coal

Medieval Methods

During the Middle Ages in Europe, bell pits were used to extract coal from the ground. They started as holes in the ground which became deeper as more coal was removed. Bell pits were as much as 8 metres deep and the miner would eventually have to use a ladder to climb down. At the bottom of the pit, the miner hollowed out the walls with a pick and hammer to extract as much coal as he could before the sides of the pit collapsed.

Coal occurs in layers beneath sedimentary rocks. It is a type of fossil fuel, made from the remains of trees and plants that grew in swampy forests millions of years ago. In time, heat, and the pressure from the growing layers of sedimentary rocks above, turned the soft plant material into solid rock. Since medieval times, coal has been mined to provide fuel.

With the introduction of steam power during the Industrial Revolution of the late eighteenth century, coal mining became easier and safer. There were pumps to supply air and remove flood water, and winding gear to take miners down in cages to great depths. But the increasing demand for coal could only be satisfied by armies of underground workers, and many of these were children.

Children had to carry baskets of coal that were many times heavier than themselves. They had to climb several ladders to reach the lift shaft with a basket on their back. Children often worked for twelve hours underground. If they fell asleep they would be beaten with a stick.

"I'm a trapper in the Gawber pit. It does not tire me, but I have to trap without a light, and I'm scared. Sometimes I sing when I have a light, but not in the dark. I dare not sing then." Sarah Gooder age 8 (*Child Labour in the Mines*, 1842). Trappers had to open and shut trapdoors that allowed clean air into the pit.

Modern Mining

By the end of the nineteeth century, motorized wagons were used to haul coal to the surface and pneumatic drills were used to cut coal from the seams. Today, countries such as South Africa use a method called 'bord and pillar' mining wherever coal deposits are not too deep. Big digging machines called road headers (see page 40) create vast underground chambers by stripping the coal seams using a rotating cutter. This leaves huge pillars of coal that support the roof.

A miner using the 'longwall' mining technique.

In the USA and Australia the 'longwall' mining technique is used. Beneath a roof supported by steel props and beams, a mechanical cutter with two large, revolving shearing drums moves along the coal face ripping the coal out onto a moving conveyor belt. Huge rams push the conveyor and the coal cutter forward, and roof supports are added as the machines move along. In the Bulga pit in Queensland, Australia, one longwall machine mined 21,160 tonnes of coal per worker in one year.

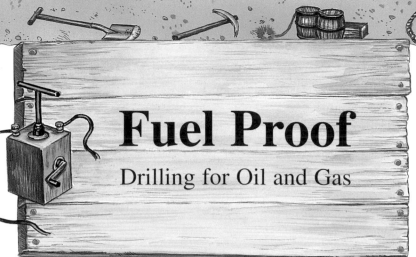

Fuel Proof

Drilling for Oil and Gas

Fossil Fuels

Oil – like gas and coal – is a fossil fuel. Fossil fuels are made from an organic substance called carbon. The formation of oil and gas took place over many millions of years. Layers of rotting plant and animal remains were covered in mud and sands which eventually turned into rock. Huge wells of natural gas or liquid oil below the rock are waiting to be discovered by explorers.

The drill on an oil rig is powered from a high steel crane called a 'derrick'. The drill itself is made up of a hollow, revolving tube with a tip of diamond-tipped teeth that are sharp enough to cut through rock. As the drill bit sinks down, the oil workers on the platform lengthen it by adding on new lengths of hollow tube. When oil is struck, it flows up inside the tube and is piped to a huge storage tank on the sea bed. Then it is transferred via pipelines or tankers to an onshore refinery where the crude (impure) oil is cleaned for use as a fuel.

Anchored to the sea bed and built from massive steel tubes and girders, this oil rig supports a drilling platform from which a hole is being bored. It is possibly as deep as 2km. Deep beneath the layers of surface rock, the drill will strike oil.

Helicopters deliver supplies to the drilling platform

Many drilling platforms are built to float so that they can move around finding new wells. They can be pulled out to sea by powerful tugs and then weighted down and anchored to the sea bed. Once oil is struck, a cap is put onto the top or 'head' of the well. The temporary platform is then ready to be refloated and towed to another drilling location to make way for a permanent platform.

Well Oiled

The first oil well was drilled at Titusville, Pennsylvania in the USA in 1859. At that time, oil was mainly used as a lubricant for machinery. Later, it was refined to produce gasolene – the fuel that powered the first cars.

Modern drilling methods mean you don't have to drill down vertically to find oil. Flexible pipes and drills that bore sideways allow oil exploration companies to drill out to sea from an oil rig on shore.

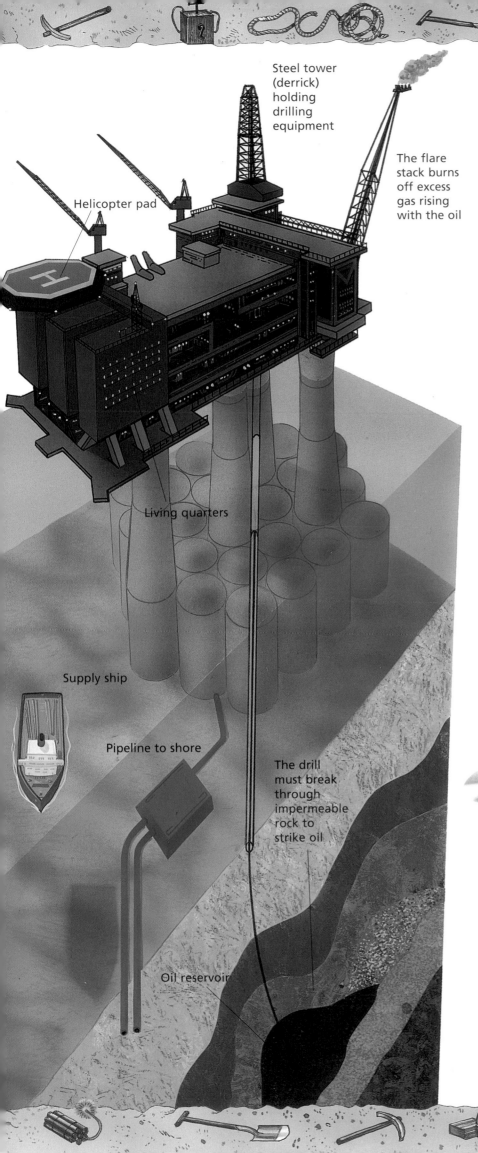

Steel tower (derrick) holding drilling equipment

The flare stack burns off excess gas rising with the oil

Helicopter pad

Living quarters

Supply ship

Pipeline to shore

The drill must break through impermeable rock to strike oil

Oil reservoir

New Finds

By studying maps of rock formations and aerial photographs, geologists can judge the likeliest places where oil and gas can be found. The biggest oil reserves are in Texas (USA), Saudi Arabia, Kuwait, Iraq, Africa, Azerbaijan and Khazakstan. The biggest undersea deposits are found in the North Sea, the Gulf of Mexico and off the coast of Newfoundland. In the future, geologists hope to discover huge oil reserves beneath the Antarctic.

Derricks called 'nodding donkeys' are used to extract oil on land.

Fuel Facts

◆ Around 2,000 years ago, the first underground oil was found accidentally by the Chinese while they were drilling for salt water.

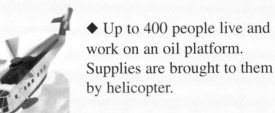

◆ Up to 400 people live and work on an oil platform. Supplies are brought to them by helicopter.

◆ The world's heaviest oil platform, *Gullfaks C* in the North Sea, weighs 846 tonnes and stands at 380m (115ft).

◆ Oil and gas are highly flammable, and drilling is dangerous work. In 1988, 167 people died in the North Sea's *Piper Alpha* disaster.

◆ Divers are used in oil exploration at depths of up to 365m (1,200ft). They wear very thick 'newt suits' that allow them to breathe air at normal pressure.

Stratagems
Treasure-hunting

The Big Hole

When South Africa was colonized by Europeans in the nineteenth century, discoveries of massive deposits of diamonds sparked a rush of prospectors, all trying to stake a claim. At Kimberley, a shallow valley was turned into a big hole as thousands of miners dug frantically. The sheer number of diamonds being found flooded the market and prices fell.

Gemstones are crystals formed in rock. Molten liquid from inside the earth's crust cools and separates in cracks of rock forming veins of sparkling, pure crystal. These stones are highly prized for their colour and for the way in which they can be cut into fashioned shapes or jewels. Gemstones are rare, and so tonnes of rock have to be dug, crushed, and sifted just to find a small quantity of crystals which may be embedded in the rocks.

Each miner at the 'Big Hole' was allowed an area of 3 metres square to mine.

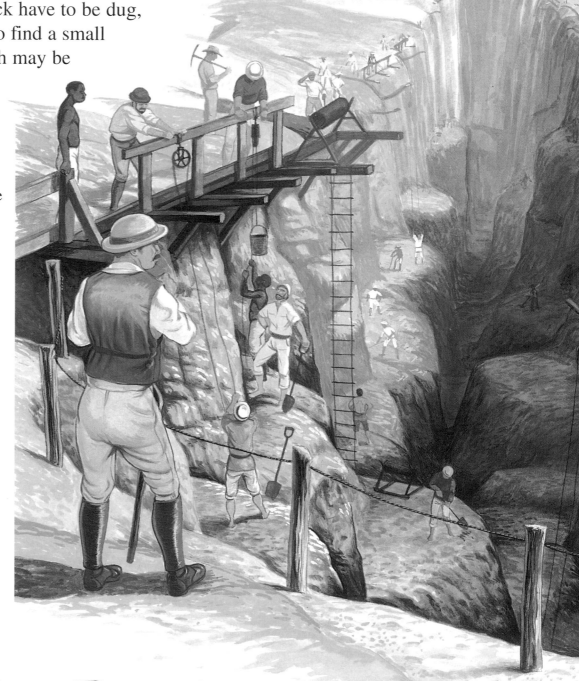

Diamonds

Diamonds are formed deep within the earth's molten core where the unimaginably high temperature – over 1000˚C – transforms carbon into pure diamond crystals. Diamonds are found in only a very few places on earth where molten rock forced its way to the earth's surface many millions of years ago.

The giant Koh-i-Noor diamond was said to have been mined at Golconda, India, in 1304. Owned by Indian princes, the huge, 108-carat gem takes its name from the Indian name for 'fountain of light'. The diamond was presented to Queen Victoria of Great Britain in 1850.

British pioneer Cecil Rhodes bought as many shares as he could in the Kimberley mine and created a stable price for the gems. In 1888, he created De Beers Consolidated Mines Ltd. – a company that exists today.

Diamond Details

◆ In some mines, as much as 95% of the diamonds are of no use as gems. They are either too rough or too small to be cut into the facets or carats that give gems their 'sparkle' (see below).

◆ Five countries produce 90% of the world's diamonds – Australia, Botswana, Namibia, South Africa and Russia.

◆ What do diamonds, coal and pencil lead have in common? They are all forms of carbon!

◆ Diamond is the hardest naturally occurring substance known. It is widely used in industry for drilling and polishing.

Diamond Cutting

1. Marking
The planner decides how the stone should be cut and marks it.

2. Sawing
The sawyer shapes the diamond into a cone shape with a thin, bronze saw.

3. Faceting 1
The 'blocker' cuts the first 'facets' on the stone with a revolving iron disc.

4. Faceting 2
The angles of the facets must be exact to ensure maximum brilliancy.

5. Finishing
The 'brillianteer' places and polishes the final facets and checks the shape.

Sand Stones

The most productive diamond mine in the world is in Namibia, southern Africa. It is a strip of beach 160-kms long. Diamonds are often found among deposits from inland volcanoes. They are washed down to the coast in rivers. Huge hydraulic excavators strip layers of sand away from the bed rock. The sand may be as deep as 25 metres. Miners will then scour the rock for loose diamonds.

Undermining the Enemy

Medieval Warfare

How easy do you think it would be for soldiers, armed with only swords and bows and arrows, to batter a hole in a 3-metre-thick stone wall? Long before gunpowder, medieval soldiers with hand tools managed to dig underneath castle walls and bring them crashing down.

The Crusades

The crusades of the 11th and 12th centuries ended the belief that castles were indestructible. Christian crusader knights from western Europe tried to defend castles in the Middle East from Muslim attackers. The Muslims were digging underneath castle walls and blowing them up.

The crusaders learned quickly. When the Muslims tried to dig mines, crusaders would listen for the sound of the digging then dig down to try to find them. Sometimes they dug into the enemy's mine and there would be fierce hand-to-hand fighting underground.

The Siege of Acre

When English king Richard the Lionheart laid siege to the walled city of Acre in north-west Israel in 1190, he bombarded it with long-range catapults for nearly a month. Meanwhile, under the cover of wooden shelters, his miners dug tunnels under the city walls to undermine them.

One crusader knight wrote: "hardly a day passed without a section collapsing into rubble with a great roar of choking dust, whereupon men rushed into the breach to fight like devils."

Burrowing under the foundations, King Richard's miners put in wooden props to support the stone wall above. When a big enough section of wall had been excavated, the miners brought in piles of brushwood and set fire to the wooden props. They ran back along the tunnel to safety, leaving the wall to collapse. Acre fell shortly afterwards.

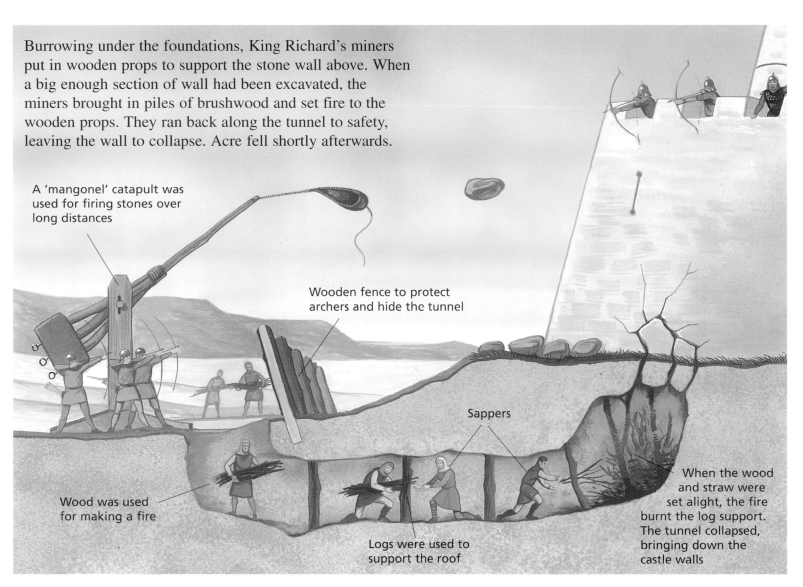

A 'mangonel' catapult was used for firing stones over long distances

Wooden fence to protect archers and hide the tunnel

Sappers

Wood was used for making a fire

Logs were used to support the roof

When the wood and straw were set alight, the fire burnt the log support. The tunnel collapsed, bringing down the castle walls

Boiling Pigs

When King John laid siege to Rochester castle in England in 1215, his miners dug a huge tunnel underneath the wall and supported the foundations on wooden props. It took them six weeks to dig a mine. After they had finished, they filled it with wood. Forty pigs were slaughtered to provide boiling fat which was poured over the wood to make it burn quickly.

Castles Under Attack

When medieval miners attacked castles they went for the weakest points. In square buildings, these were the corners where two walls met. Gradually, castle builders realized that they had to build round castles where the wall would support itself. Builders also laid bigger, deeper stone foundations through which it was impossible to tunnel. Of course, the best castles were the ones built on top of solid rock!

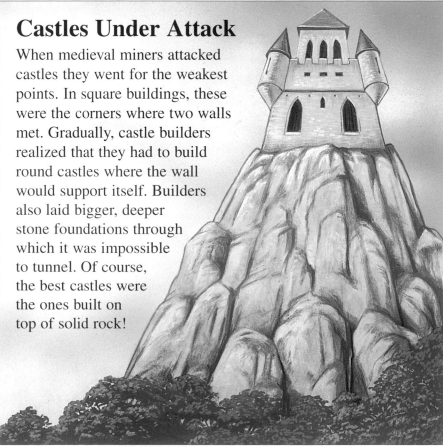

No Man's Land

Trench Warfare

During the First World War, miners were urgently needed in the army. When war broke out, the cavalry – soldiers mounted on horseback – were the most important fighters. But the first battles, such as the Battle of Mons in Belgium, created confusion and resulted in a great loss of men, horses and equipment. The German and Allied armies began digging defensive earthworks called 'trenches' around the positions they held.

The Trenches

Once lines of trenches had been dug, the next most important thing was to excavate living quarters and command posts. These were called 'dug-outs' and the miners who were commissioned to do the digging were known as 'sappers'. They tunnelled 8 metres below the level of the trench and reinforced the roof with steel bars, concrete and sand bags.

On the Western Front, lines of trenches were dug all the way from the Swiss border to the Belgian coast. On one section of the front line at Lens in northern France, Australian and Canadian tunnellers dug a series of tunnels up to 23m underground. An electric railway carried ammunition to troops along that part of the line. The Germans built very strong tunnels that were lined with concrete.

Secret Weapon

Once inside the trenches and dug outs, soldiers were safe from snipers' bullets and shellfire. But each of the armies wielded a secret weapon. Sappers dug tunnels from their own trenches towards the enemy lines to plant explosives underneath them. The end of the tunnel was filled with explosive which could be set off by a detonator wired up to a tiny generator box. Pushing the plunger down on the generator box sent a tiny electric current, sparking the detonator and setting off the explosive charge.

"A stairway of some thirty rough steps led down to a chamber where there was an air pump and a windlass. From this chamber a tunnel ran right under the German front lines... This is not war it is wholesale butchery, for in a mine they put up to 100 tons of ammonal – enough to blow a thousand men to pieces!"

(Private J Bowles, Queen's Westminster Rifles)

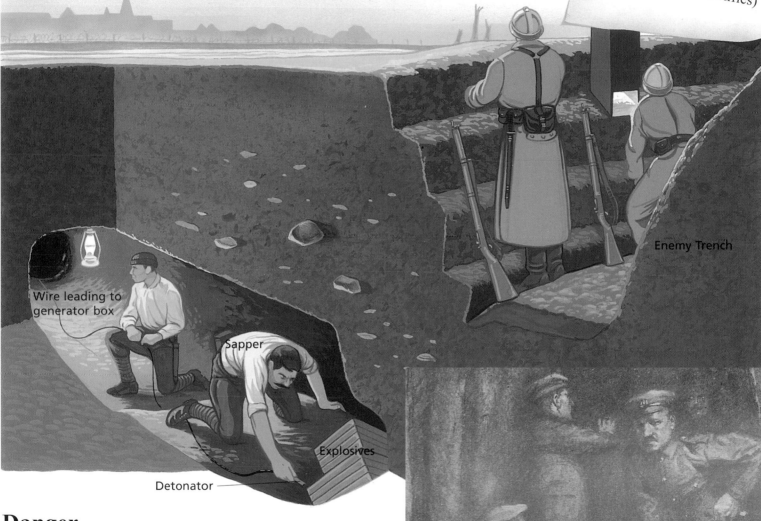

Enemy Trench

Wire leading to generator box

Sapper

Explosives

Detonator

Danger

Sappers worked in shifts to dig tunnels by hand out of soft clay. Sometimes men were killed when tunnels collapsed. To prevent this, the sappers shored up the tunnel sides and roof with wooden boards and props.

There was also the constant danger that the enemy would hear the sappers tunnelling, undermine their position and blow them up. As a result, tunnels had listening posts where sappers put their ears to the ground to listen out for faint noises of enemy digging.

This picture appeared in *The War Illustrated* in October 1917. It shows a sapper using a detection device to try and locate enemy activity.

TUNNELS
Sheltered Accommodation

Safety Underground

The development of airships and aircraft in the early years of the twentieth century brought warfare closer to civilian populations. In both major world wars, bombing raids wreaked havoc in cities and towns. People sheltered from the bombs wherever they could and railway tunnels were an ideal hiding place.

In London, all tube trains came to a standstill during a raid. People bought the cheapest tickets they could and slept huddled together on draughty platforms. They brought their own bedding with them and small suitcases filled with their possessions. The Underground became a home to people whose houses had been destroyed in the bombing. There were no toilets, so people had to use buckets. Eventually, the British Government converted the Underground into an official public shelter and put in bunk-beds and chemical lavatories.

The Blitz

In 1940, European cities and ports were targeted by the German air force in night-time bombing raids. The Blitz, named after the German 'Blitzkrieg' (lightning war), became a part of everyday life.

Families huddled together in iron shelters they had built in their gardens called Anderson shelters. In European cities, deep railway tunnels offered the best protection.

Underground Command

During World War Two, Winston Churchill, his ministers and chiefs of staff were based in a command centre deep in the basement of a government building in London's Whitehall (right). Below ground, the underground network of 200 war rooms and offices were protected by a 5-metre-thick concrete roof which was reinforced with steel rails.

German war leader, Adolf Hitler and his generals spent the last days of the war planning their last ditch battle from an underground bunker in Berlin. By April 1945 the Russian army entered the outskirts of Berlin. On May 1 1945, it is believed that Hitler committed suicide in the bunker.

Winston Churchill's underground command centre

In From The Cold

The Cold War between the United States, Russia and their allies, begun in the 1950s, brought a new threat. Both sides developed nuclear missiles that could destroy entire populations with radiation. Governments built deep-level underground command centres equipped with secure phone lines. With the first warning of a nuclear attack, heads of state and officials would be transported via secret underground tunnels to the safety of a deep shelter.

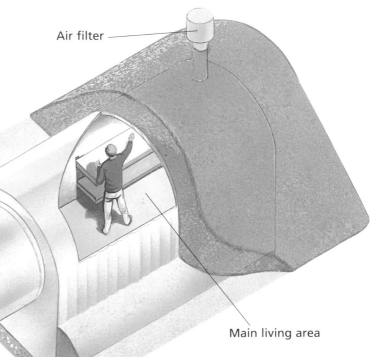

Air filter

Main living area

Steel nuclear shelters were sunk into the ground and covered with earth.

Entrance to shelter

Private underground fall-out shelters like the one pictured would have housed a family of six for many months until the radioactivity levels declined.

Undercover Combat

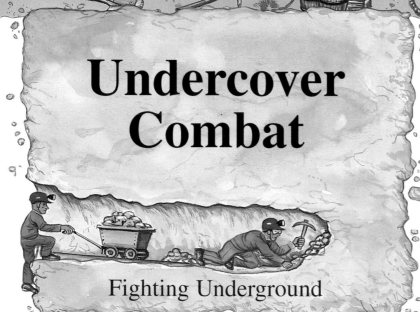

Fighting Underground

The Tunnels of Cu Chi

The Cu Chi tunnels took many, many years to dig in the soft clay of South Vietnam. Digging began when the country was under French rule; the tunnels were first used as bolt-holes for Vietnamese rebels evading capture. Between 1955 and 1975, US soldiers were attempting to protect South Vietnam from communist guerillas from the north. They were fighting an unseen enemy.

The Viet Cong or 'VC' lived and fought from the Cu Chi tunnels. US army patrols were ambushed by snipers who would then escape down a concealed trapdoor into an underground labyrinth. With many kilometres of tunnels, VC guerillas could appear anywhere without warning.

During wartime, underground passages have been used by soldiers and civilians to surprise their enemies or to escape from them. Imagine hiding in a confined space where you could be buried alive by a cave-in, or trapped and killed by a watchful enemy.

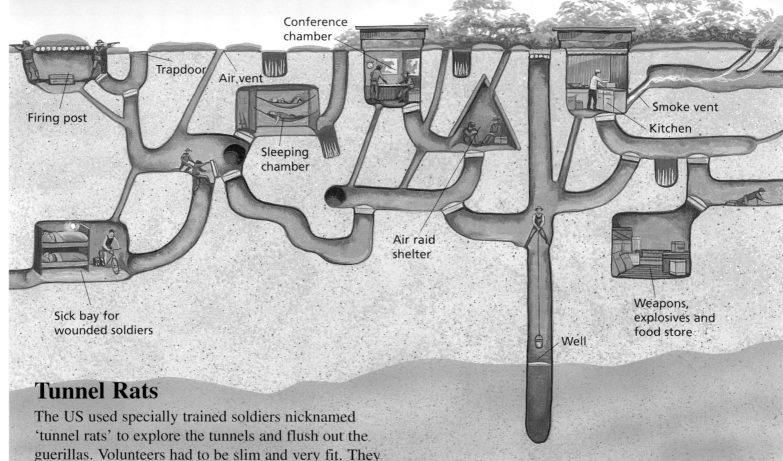

Conference chamber

Trapdoor

Air vent

Firing post

Sleeping chamber

Smoke vent

Kitchen

Air raid shelter

Sick bay for wounded soldiers

Weapons, explosives and food store

Well

Tunnel Rats

The US used specially trained soldiers nicknamed 'tunnel rats' to explore the tunnels and flush out the guerillas. Volunteers had to be slim and very fit. They also had to have nerves of steel. There was not enough space for a tunnel rat to turn round so if he met a VC in the tunnel he either had to kill or be killed.

The Wooden Horse

During World War Two, Allied airmen inside German prison camp Stalag Luft III were fighting their own war. They used their prison exercise time to dig an escape tunnel 40 metres long! While Stalag prisoners jumped over a wooden exercise horse, one man beneath it burrowed in the soft sand. When he was finished, he put a trapdoor over the tunnel entrance and threw sand on top to camouflage it. Then, he hung the bags of excavated sand on hooks inside the hollow horse. Finally, he crouched up inside it and was carried away to the hut where the exercise horse was kept.

The tunnels of Cu Chi were home to real rats and fire ants. The VC often left booby traps underground – anything from a box of scorpions to a nail bomb. After a narrow escape, a tunnel rat might be so terrified that he would never go underground again.

Guard watch tower

Wire security fence

Cross-section through the vaulting horse

Bags of excavated sand

Loose boards were placed over the tunnel entrance and covered with sand

Tunnel shaft supported with bricks

Boards taken from prison huts supported the tunnel sides

Human Moles

The plan was to dig an escape route under the prison wire. Digging was dirty, dangerous work. The men worked in suffocating conditions. As the tunnel got longer, one man pulled a sledge full of soil back along the tunnel while the other dug. It was a race to finish the tunnel before it was discovered by the eagle-eyed German sentries.

After three months, three Allied airmen made their escape armed with false identity papers and German money. They carried bundles of homemade civilian clothes to disguise themselves. With the help of Polish resistance workers, the escapees made their way across occupied Europe and boarded a ship bound for neutral Sweden.

Boring Work

Underwater Tunnelling

The problem of tunnelling under a river bed had puzzled the world's engineering minds for centuries. The tunnel could easily collapse in on the diggers if water was not prevented from seeping in. Nineteenth-century inventor Marc Brunel built the world's first river tunnel using an ingenious, new device. . .

The Thames Tunnel

Before the days of railways and motorways, rivers were busy trade routes. During the early nineteenth century, London's sailing ships brought trade and wealth to the city but their tall masts meant that bridges could not be built along the River Thames. Brunel's idea was to build a tunnel under the river so that people and goods could travel from one side of the city to the other.

In March 1825, Brunel used a rather odd method to sink his first shaft. He built a massive brick tower high above the ground. The tower had walls one metre thick. As more and more bricks were added, so the tower got heavier and heavier, until finally it started to sink into the marshy ground under its own weight. Inside the brick-lined shaft, miners dug while a steam engine pumped water out and helped lift buckets of soil to the surface.

Brunel discovered a way of tunnelling through soft earth using an iron shield to prevent the roof caving in. As the shield was inched forward, bricklayers following on behind built an arched tunnel lining to take the weight of the earth above.

Steam engine

Buckets of soil and water were winched to the surface of the shaft.

Brick-lined shaft

Disaster!

The conditions under the Thames were difficult. Miners had to follow a thin band of clay. If they went below it they would hit quicksand, if they went above it, then they risked being flooded. Brunel's miners were protected by a tunnelling shield as they hacked at the clay with picks and shovels. For two years all went well. Then disaster struck when the tunnel was midway beneath the river. The earth wall at the head of the tunnel burst and the river came flooding in.

Repairing the Damage

One miner was drowned but Brunel was determined not to be beaten. He hired a diving bell (an enclosed steel chamber with glass portholes) to inspect the river bed. He found that dredgers had been scraping mud and gravel from the river bed to make it deeper for cargo boats. The roof of the tunnel was now just a few feet below the river bed. Brunel filled up the hole with sacks of clay, pumped out the water, and continued digging. A year later, a second flood killed six workers. Brunel finally decided to call a halt.

The Tunnel Completed

Brunel's company had run out of money, but the government decided that London needed a tunnel and in 1835 lent Brunel enough money to finish it. In March 1843, the construction opened as a foot tunnel. Brunel's original idea for a road tunnel had to be abandoned due to lack of money. In all, the 365-metre tunnel had taken twenty years to complete. Brunel's tunnel is still in use today as a tunnel for underground trains.

Iron tunnelling shield

A 'travelling stage' transported men and debris along the tunnel.

The tunnel face was secured with wooden boards.

Metromania

The First Underground

"The sound of pickaxes, spades and hammers, puffing of steam and murmur of voices begin, never to cease day or night." (John Hollingshead, 1860). This was the scene in London in 1860 when work started on The Metropolitan Railway – the world's first underground railway. The tunnel was dug by 'cut and cover', a method which involved cutting a deep trench then covering it over with bricks and earth.

The Metropolitan railway followed the line of a road which was dug up by teams of labourers. These men were called 'navvies' after the workers who dug canals or 'navigations'. Working only with picks and shovels, the navvies slowly excavated a deep 'cutting' (trench), using timber props to keep the sides from collapsing. When the cutting was deep enough, teams of bricklayers lined the sides with a thick skin of brick and then built an arch between the walls.

Closing streets and digging them up was no easy task in a big city. Drains, sewers and gas pipes had to be diverted. Sometimes houses had to be demolished as well. The Metropolitan railway opened in London in 1863.

To create an arch, bricks were laid on wooden frames which provided a temporary support. Afterwards the earth was filled back on top of the arch and the road was relaid.

When electric trains began to replace steams trains in the 1890s, it meant that tunnels could be much deeper. The Greathead tunnelling shield, invented in 1869, protected tunnellers from cave-ins, enabling them to work at greater depths. John Price's drum tunnel boring machine, invented in 1897, enabled tunnels to be dug faster and more safely than ever before. Virtually every European city began to build their own underground rail network.

The Moscow Underground

Marble halls, crystal chandeliers and elaborate murals. No, these are not the contents of a stately home but are typical station decorations on Russia's famous Moscow Metro. The first section of the Moscow Metro between Sokolniki and Gorki Park was built in 1935 using cut and cover construction. The sumptuous decor was designed to impress foreign visitors and to be a celebration of communism's power to the people.

Today the Moscow Metro carries more passengers than any other underground railway in the world – a total of 2,500 million passenger journeys per year.

Rapid Transit

The construction techniques used to build modern metro systems differ little from early methods, except that the digging is carried out by modern tunnelling machines and excavators. However, one of the most exciting recent developments is the driverless train.

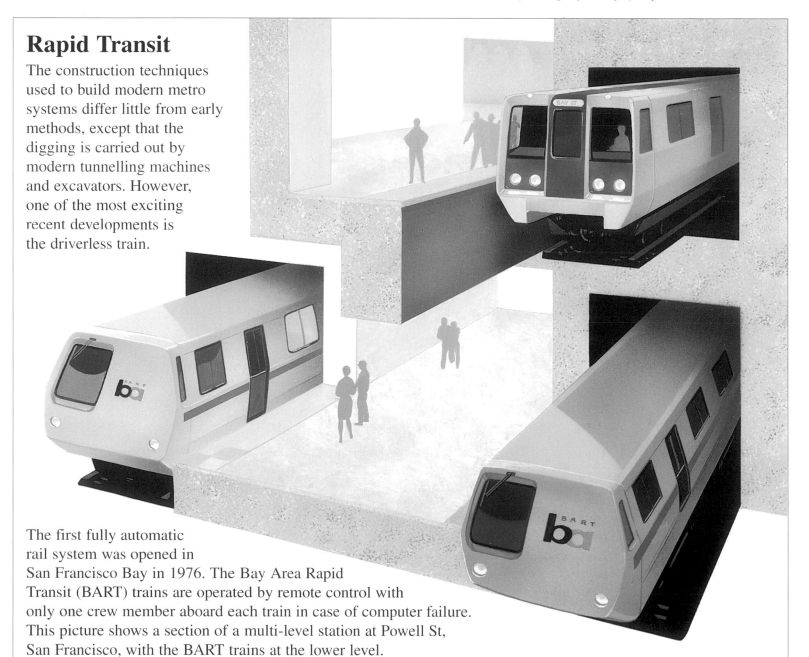

The first fully automatic rail system was opened in San Francisco Bay in 1976. The Bay Area Rapid Transit (BART) trains are operated by remote control with only one crew member aboard each train in case of computer failure. This picture shows a section of a multi-level station at Powell St, San Francisco, with the BART trains at the lower level.

Tunnel Vision

Modern Tunnelling Projects

People no longer rely on sea or air travel to transport them around wide stretches of water. Road and rail tunnels make convenient short cuts, particularly when the distances are quite small. Among the projected schemes of the future are a tunnel from southern Spain to North Africa, and a tunnel linking Alaska to Russia.

The Channel Tunnel

British and French engineers have been putting forward plans for a linking tunnel between their countries for nearly 200 years. Early proposals came up against strong protests and technical difficulties. Following another failed attempt in 1975, thousands of construction workers started digging two rail tunnels and a service tunnel in June 1988 at Shakespeare Cliff in England. On the opposite side of the English Channel at Sangatte, French teams were digging towards England. The aim was to meet up 50 metres beneath the sea bed in the middle of the Channel.

Cross-section showing the three tunnels that now run under the English channel

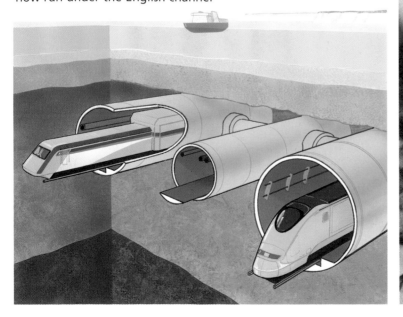

Dangerous Digging

Working in a confined space with huge tunnel boring machines (TBMs) was very dangerous and slow to begin with. Over the course of the project, ten construction workers were killed.

Cutterhead

In December 1990 British and French tunnellers broke through and shook hands across the joined-up tunnel. It was the first time people could walk from one side of the Channel to the other since the Ice Age, when the sea level was far lower than it is today.

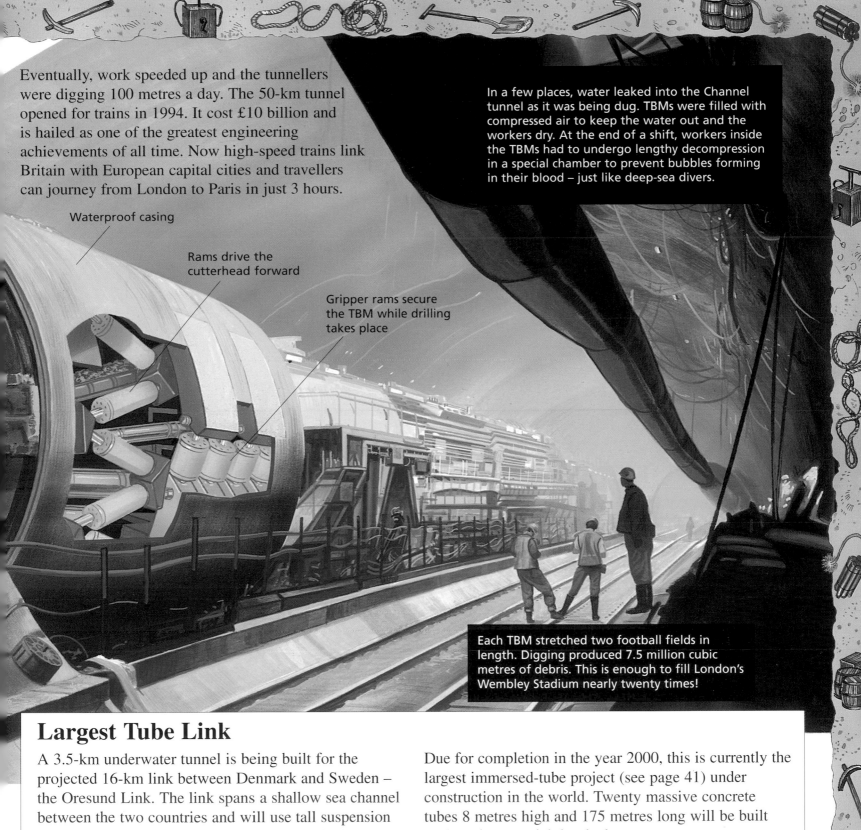

Eventually, work speeded up and the tunnellers were digging 100 metres a day. The 50-km tunnel opened for trains in 1994. It cost £10 billion and is hailed as one of the greatest engineering achievements of all time. Now high-speed trains link Britain with European capital cities and travellers can journey from London to Paris in just 3 hours.

Waterproof casing

Rams drive the cutterhead forward

Gripper rams secure the TBM while drilling takes place

In a few places, water leaked into the Channel tunnel as it was being dug. TBMs were filled with compressed air to keep the water out and the workers dry. At the end of a shift, workers inside the TBMs had to undergo lengthy decompression in a special chamber to prevent bubbles forming in their blood – just like deep-sea divers.

Each TBM stretched two football fields in length. Digging produced 7.5 million cubic metres of debris. This is enough to fill London's Wembley Stadium nearly twenty times!

Largest Tube Link

A 3.5-km underwater tunnel is being built for the projected 16-km link between Denmark and Sweden – the Oresund Link. The link spans a shallow sea channel between the two countries and will use tall suspension bridges, artificial islands and tunnels along its length.

Due for completion in the year 2000, this is currently the largest immersed-tube project (see page 41) under construction in the world. Twenty massive concrete tubes 8 metres high and 175 metres long will be built onshore in a special dry dock.

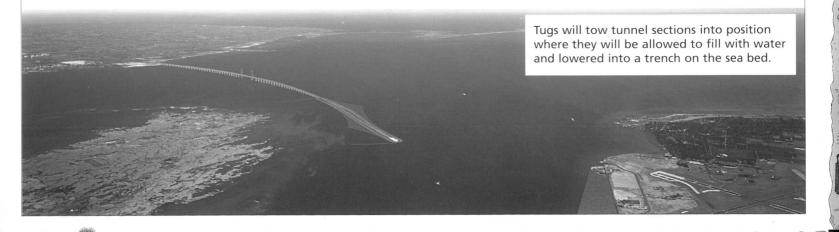

Tugs will tow tunnel sections into position where they will be allowed to fill with water and lowered into a trench on the sea bed.

Machinations

Modern Tunnelling Technology

S peed, accuracy and safety are the keys to modern tunnelling technology. Modern machines dig faster and are usually safer than the old manual methods. Tunnels can be built more quickly and use less workers underground. With only one operator at the controls, a modern machine replaces armies of labourers with picks and shovels.

Drill and Blast

Tunnelling under mountains where the rock is very hard calls for a method called 'drill and blast'. Tunnellers bore holes in the rock face with a drilling jumbo – a series of giant drills mounted on a moveable carriage. The drillbits are tipped with a metal called tungsten carbide which can bore through the hardest rock. Guided by computer, the drill operator makes a precise pattern of holes which are then filled with explosive to blast out the rock.

In earlier days, rock blasting brought the danger of tunnel collapse. Today's civil engineers solve the problem by installing anchors – long stainless steel bolts designed to stabilize the rock face. The expanding anchor bolts are inserted into specially drilled holes.

Drilling Jumbo

NATM

Road Header

NATM

Tunnels through rock are made safer with the New Austrian Tunnelling Method (NATM). Sections of steel mesh are placed on the walls and roof of the tunnel and are then sprayed with fast-drying liquid concrete called shotcrete. This hardens to provide a strong support. Sometimes, the tunnel is reinforced with further concrete lining sections.

Immersed Tube Tunnelling

Some river crossings are too tricky for conventional tunnelling methods, so huge concrete tunnel sections are used. The sections are cast in a dry dock,

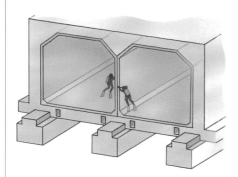

sealed and made watertight. When the dry dock is flooded, the sections float and can be towed into position on the river crossing by tugs. Held in place by cranes on barges, the tunnel sections are slowly filled with water. After they have sunk to the bottom, the 'immersed tube' sections are bolted together by divers.

Road Headers

Road headers are also used for tunnelling. These machines move on caterpillar tracks. A revolving cutter head on the end of a long metal arm tears into the tunnel face. The driver presses a lever to operate big hydraulic rams that raise or lower the cutter arm. As the road header moves forward, a tiny bulldozer blade sweeps debris onto a conveyor belt which feeds it onto a skip wagon.

TBM

TBMs

Tunnel boring machines or TBMs are suited to soft ground or rock. A huge cylinder cuts out the full diameter of the tunnel in one go as a revolving cutter scoops rock from the work face. Debris is fed through holes in the cutting head onto a conveyor belt. It is then taken to a waiting rail skip. The body of the TBM is a tunnelling shield designed to support the roof of the tunnel as it is being dug. Inside the shield, tunnellers work in safety, moving the shield forward by lifting it with powerful jacks (see page 38).

Dig This!

French engineers pioneered the drill and blast method when the 13.6-km Mont Cenis rail tunnel under the Alps was completed in 1871. The tunnel took 14 years to dig.

Immersed tube tunnels were first used in the U.S. in 1906 when lengths of steel tube encased in concrete were linked under the Detroit River to create a rail tunnel.

The longest immersed tube tunnel in the world is the Bay Area Rapid Transit Tunnel in San Francisco, U.S. It opened in 1974 and is 5.8km long.

In 1995 the world's biggest TBMs began tunnelling the 15-km Trans Tokyo Bay highway in Japan. The machines have a diameter of 14.4m and weigh 3,150 tonnes. A robot fits together eleven 10-tonne concrete tunnel segments in just 100 minutes to form a complete ring section.

Secret Services

Support Networks

Tunnels are needed for a range of underground services such as power supply, water supply, drainage, and the storage of nuclear waste. A vast underground jungle exists under the streets of New York. The city's network of underground services is the most complex in the world. There are 215km of subway, 9,656km of sewer, 125,528km of gas mains, 99,779km of electrical cable, and 500,000 manhole covers. There are also many abandoned nineteenth-century tunnels, some of which are completely uncharted.

Steam Scene

The city streets are heated by a complex of nineteenth-century steam pipes which keep snow at bay in winter. The pipes are leaky, and jets of steam sometimes blow up to the sidewalk through open vents. One of the most famous scenes from movie history comes from the film *The Seven Year Itch* where the actress Marilyn Monroe holds on to the hem of her skirt to prevent it being lifted by a jet of steam!

Skyscrapers

When construction of the Empire State Building started in 1929 in New York, workers started digging downwards. This was to build massive foundations needed to support the building. A hole 17-metres deep was dug to form the basement levels. Below this, engineers bored holes that were filled with concrete and steel reinforcements down to the bedrock. Over 200 concrete and steel 'piles' support the building.

New York's tallest building, the 110-storey World Trade Center, is equally impressive below ground. Under the skyscraper is a vast underground concourse lined with shops and restaurants.

Water Supply

New York could run dry next century but not if its new water supply tunnel is finished on time. The city needs 6.5 billion litres of water a day.

The new 96-km tunnel will encircle the city and draw water from reservoirs to the north and south of the city. There are already two water supply tunnels but a third is needed to cope with growing demand and to provide emergency back-up in case one tunnel has to be closed for repairs.

The tunnellers are cutting through bedrock 240m below ground level. The 7m-diameter tunnel is being excavated by drill and blast and is lined with fast-drying spray concrete (see page 40). Work on the tunnel started in 1970 but will not be complete until 2009 .

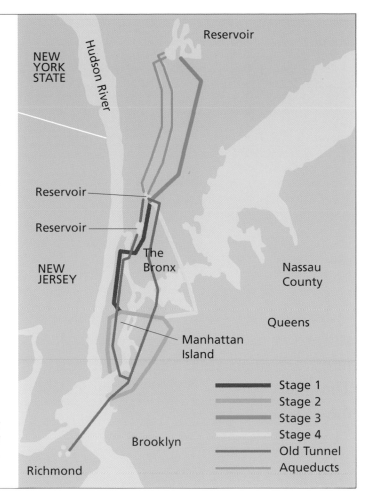

The New York water supply tunnel is being built in four stages over nearly 40 years.

Legend:
- Stage 1
- Stage 2
- Stage 3
- Stage 4
- Old Tunnel
- Aqueducts

Map labels: NEW YORK STATE, Hudson River, Reservoir, Reservoir, Reservoir, The Bronx, NEW JERSEY, Nassau County, Queens, Manhattan Island, Brooklyn, Richmond

Lesotho Highlands Water Project

One of the world's biggest tunnelling projects will not only supply water but generate hydro-electric power as well. Started in 1986, the 78-km Lesotho Highlands water tunnel in South Africa will will take thirty years to complete.

When finished, the tunnel will carry water from the Orange River in Lesotho to feed a series of five dams where water pressure will drive turbines. These will generate enough electricity to supply Lesotho's entire energy needs. The water will eventually supply cities in South Africa.

Glossary

alloy a mixture of two or more chemical elements, at least one of which is metal

carat A measure of the purity of gold; pure gold is 24 carats

coal-seam a layer of coal that is suitable for mining

decompression a gradual reduction of air pressure on a diver who has been subjected to high pressure underwater

detonator a small electrical device used to set off an explosive

dredger a machine used for lifting objects from the mud and silt of the sea bed

drill bit the tip of a drill

excavate to excavate something is to dig it up

facet one side of a cut gemstone which has many sides cut into it

fossil fuel a fuel such as coal or gas which has been formed over millions of years from the remains of plants and animals

generator a machine that converts mechanical energy into electrical energy

hydraulic describes a machine that operates by transferring pressure through a liquid

Ice Age a period in the earth's history when ice sheets covered the land. The most recent ice age occurred 1,800,000 years ago

lava hot, molten (liquid) rock that flows from volcanoes

mineral a chemical that occurs naturally inside rocks

ore rock that contains metals

organic describes a compound (a substance made up of two or more elements) that contains carbon

overburden a layer of rock that must be removed before minerals can be mined beneath it

pneumatic drill a powerful drill driven by compressed air, used for breaking up a hard surface such as rock

radiation a way in which heat energy is sent out in electromagnetic waves

refinery a place where impurities are removed from crude oil

sedimentary rock rocks that formed in layers

shaft a long, vertical, narrow space used to enter a mine

smelt to extract metal from ore by melting it

Index